Labi Siffre

BLOOD
ON THE
PAGE

GW00771069

A Xavier Book

First published in 1995
by Xavier Books
P.O. Box 17 Abergavenny Gwent NP8 1XA

LEGAL NOTICE

ISBN   0-9520942-1-5

Book Design by *Valleys Artworks*
9 Lanelay Terrace, Maesycoed,
Pontypridd, Mid Glamorgan, CF37 1ER

Printed in Great Britain by
Zenith Treforest Press Limited
Mid Glamorgan

poetry by the same author
on Xavier Books

NIGGER

•

representation:
Earth Music
0181-677-9331

Acknowledgements

With thanks to: Eric Hands at *Earth Music*, Peter Lloyd at Xavier Books, Odetta, Janice Ginsberg, John Evans, Sue Rees, and *Noumena Writers*.

In remembrance of my brother Brian, who, close to the end, was the wisest of us all; and also in remembrance of Mary Boys.

For PJCL as always

Contents

Take no prisoners
Not even yourself

Go where everyone
tells you not to

Go where you yourself
are afraid

Safety wins no place
in the pantheon of passion

We need more guns

And while the blood flows
Fill your pen from the wound

And write

Thirty Years After the Dream

(New York - August '93)

I came from the land of grey men in faceless suits
to New York where we make as much noise as we wish
In the knowledge that no one is listening
which is probably for the best as

every one here is Numero Uno they tell each other
constantly kick arse get the fuck out'a my case
Mother nobody here takes any shit!

In a synthesis of people who believe their own myth
(as most of us do) 'though for many that myth
was written by the enemy; This makes me feel at home
being gay and black so *twice* denied *my*-story

•

Heroic
on the steps
of The Museum
of Natural History
Theodore Roosevelt rides
to the future magnificent leading
a Native-American (once better dead)
and an Afro-American (naturally bred to be herded)

Good Theodore seems to be saving them (but from who?)
and they seem trusting and grateful is this
what harmony depends upon?...a very short memory

•

At the top of the park (where the Black starts)
I spoke of this to Odetta who smiled a never surrender
smile of regret; She sings the pain of slavery and loss
better than anyone else I know
and wears this lesson on her breast

I AM

(a lesson thieves would have the dispossessed forget)

She raises her buttocks
gently
to accommodate his anxiety

this is love this giving
everything he's ever needed
when his everything
'though lovingly given
is less than she had prayed for

he breathes faster pounding away
synchronised she moves
with and against him
eager enough to display desire
she is careful not to threaten
with expectation

this time he'll come
she will make certain of it
while his helplessness without her
their mutual understanding of this
makes her want him more

Later under a younger athlete
she thinks of *him*
and smiles deciding
that that night she will make
an extra special steak and kidney pie
with dark beer and red wine
inseparable
they will eat this
his favourite meal

and nothing
of importance
will change

The child burns with fever
A mine took it's leg
In the land of decisions the warriors
dig more graves

The old woman (knowing her place)
holds her tongue
another child walks the same path

Through Swiss-cheese
scenery of de-constructed farmland
where a young girl lies
head and breasts scattered around

her legs a peace sign
with blood at the point
the warriors march with a lighter step
towards the next battle

In a low-rise town where the dogs
don't bark
and the elders tell fearsome stories
to frighten themselves in the dark
the drunkard is led to the altar sobbing
"I'm sorry, I'm sorry," again and again
but strong enough yet to refuse to accept
the mark of the lord
Alone in the crowd the old woman
laughs out loud

Feeling her breath on his tongue
a young man looks up from his task
of re-arranging excuses
loses her shadow as the old woman
steps behind the white dove curtain

where the sea, the land
    (our Mother and Father) burn
the grass, the trees (our kin) wither away
        the rivers (our blood) run with our blood

The jacket trousers vest pants and shoes are full
of the raven haired wide eyed earth skinned girl
as she hangs by the neck from the towel suspended
neat from the sky-framed rod of iron   Dying
but strong enough yet to reject the spoiling floor
She has
the power of those who have none
and someone
is holding her hand

The old woman
smiling
says

"Welcome"

There's a poet I know
drinks too much
writes good stuff
and I
like him

but one poetry date in the bar merry he said
"How ya doin' you old queen"
"Come on you old poof"
presuming this
was a chummy way
to talk with me
'cause I'm gay

Later I
manoeuvred the evening and drove him home
and on his balcony over
a glass of wine said
"DON'T EVER
TALK TO ME
LIKE THAT
AGAIN"

"Like what?"
he protested he'd never said
those words
and anyway if he had
it hadn't meant disrespect

but I
assured him he had
and it did
and I warned him again
so's he'd never forget
and after a few more drinks and him
reminiscing
'bout women he'd loved
but mislaid

he broke down and cried in my arms
drunk unshaved tired middle aged

and I held him safe
like he wanted me to
and I left him to sleep
like he wanted me to
and yes
if he'd wanted me too
I might
have stayed

and he
still drinks too much
still writes good stuff
and I
still like him

but I'm tired of straights
and their mountain top arrogance

that's all

I wonder what happened to Alan B
I fell in love with him
In Lower Four C
and he felt something good about me

We'd sit together whenever we could
In class in break or on the bus
Hip to hip never saying a word
Thigh to thigh
through grey flannel trousers sharing
a secret world

We never held hands (didn't dare that)
I was slim bright and searching
and fast as a cat
He was blue eyed wide clever and solid
with some puppy fat

and for several terms we acted out this play
'till one lunch-break-time
in a group of our friends he said

"You're a bloody queer!"

and punched me in the belly
I just walked away
                    •

The only black kid in a white boys school
I'd had to fight older and bigger than me
after which   as I'd won   or fought to a stand-still
no one bothered me ('cept the teachers)

But that day
as the sun said "Time to move on"
With my fists ever ready
the funny thing was
It never occurred to me

to hit
Alan B

and soon I'll be fifty
and so will he

I wonder
if he
thinks of me

I wonder what happened
to Alan B

The dead we've loved never leave us
haunt our dreaming
waking sleeping
haunt our needing

The dead we've loved won't come back
nor return that part of us
that waits
long after the appointed time

The dead we've loved unexpected
visit at the dinner table
when we're laughing with friends
who ask the stillness, "are you alright?"

The dead we've loved are cruel and heartless
hurt us always always hurt us
so we wander
empty helpless
wanting always wanting

You cannot give me freedom
I have always been free
these prison walls
the boundaries
of *your* captivity

You fed the soil
with my black blood
with my black bones
you ploughed the earth

And now you say
you never meant
to hurt me
never doubted my worth

Well...
I will not forgive
and I will not forget
but we must live together
or die
foolishly
and so

I offer my hand,
if not in friendship
then in hope
that your words
are worth more
than your history

You cannot give me freedom
I have always been free
Freedom lives
in me

It's a thirteenth century shipyard
boatyard? anyway I'm impressed
the brown and grey
stone looks alive
we hardly ever do that
nowadays
most of what we build is dead

Like upside down fishhooks inside this place
a forest of question marks arch
over mankind's *special relationship* with the sea
fishing boats, a galley, three elephants wide
a lifetime long,
and wooden submarines like giant fish
dreaming

Outside in the courtyard
sunbathing leaves and pink fingered flowers
calm in the cool of a lily pool
as we rest on a wooden bench and watch
an American couple squabbling like starlings

He's lost her aged mother "Jeeze
you haven't left her
wandering around on her own!?"
I have visions
of an old crone rampaging Goth
two handed axe aloft reducing
priceless galleon models
to matchwood

The man hurries off
returns petulant
She's in the toilet
The staff are complaining

They want to close up and go home is he
his mother-in-law's keeper

ever conscious of the weight

of the rock hard limes in the branches above us
I'm writing this and Peter says "sorry"
for "wittering on" about Aragon and Catalonia,
Isabella, Ferdinand, Castile, the count-dukes
of Barcelona and how
the Spanish spent 600 years
wrestling their land
back
from the Arabs who gave us
algebra
the un-number zero
and allowed
freedom of religion
('though not, I suspect,
the freedom to have none)

I like to hear him in full flow
the shining one
in our family of two
he knows a great deal of history
                    and now
he's telling me about Lepanto
the last battle fought using galleys

Our love has grown with our waistlines
and after
all those years
he knows me better than anyone:
so I guess he thinks I'll fill this poem
with the pain
of eight hundred slaves
chained
eight to an oar under sunny skies
and clouds of arrows

as they row
with their feet in the stink
of their shit and piss
and now
I have

If all of the idle
work-shy
shiftless
ne'er do well
hand out
welfare trash
pulled themselves up
by their bootstraps
like you and I did
through steadfast initiative
courage and grit;
where would we decent
hard
working folk
live

They'd be in our homes

in our jobs

taking *our* vacations!

So fuck the poor first
or third world
walk on by
better still
kill the bastards
for the sake of your kids;
keep in mind
your old age
and your family's meagre
take from the finite cake

Be Warned
never give those unwashed
whinging
spineless
ingrate turds
a break

"SUCK IT!" he shouts,
"HEY BABE! SUCK THIS BIG DICK!"
The combatants meet
on 14th and crowded
sticky heat street

In skin tight and heels she screams
"SIT ON THIS,
CHICKEN SHIT"
and gives him the finger
wrapped in barbed wire

she angers in flames
through the citizen maze
he plays
"BaBY HeY BaBe
        SiT YOur LiPS
                WHeRe iT HiTS..."

•

He's a regular guy
easy home in the comforting
Mom and Dad well watered
lawn or vacation beach
twelve year old foot-balling
son pretty six year old
summer dress daughter floss
candy wife smile by his side

He's a Joe in control
grinning friends beside
the pack keeping pace
with a desperate prey
in a game of easy
casual lay
we can drag this one down
a-n-y-time-we-want

And their laughter snaps
and snarls around her
pulling and shoving
mouths hanging on
his words on the tip
of his smiling wet tongue
burn their way through
and under the heat
grab her breasts
tearing meat
from her stomach
RAM
sandpaper punishment
between her legs
 "HHEY MOMMA
COME ON
SUCK MY JUICY BIG DICK"

No laughing now
he hates the bitch
as she hates
the helplessness
more than she hates the creep
on 14th and crowded
sticky heat street

Dead in the sun
If one of them
had had a gun.

Believing he knows more of me
than I do

In tones exasperated, plaintive,
laced with "I'm a friend"
"you can level with me"
"no need to pretend"
and "surely you *must* agree"

He probes as we dine
"Don't you find *that* attractive?"
conspiracy nodding at the workout body
of the Vogue faced waitress
in skintight and cleavage

"Not sexually", pausing mid-steak, I reply

"But I'd go for *that*"
as a solid brick shithouse
almost wide as tall
with a cue ball top
salt and pepper framed smile
rolls out of the kitchen
to cool view for a while

My foe shakes his head over 'Fish of the Day'

I don't shake mine
I'm bored having been
a prisoner mired
in his
wasteland
for most of my
life

People
are punch your teeth in
proudest of
the things over which
they've had no control
like being

White, Black, British, American, a man,
whatever...

proud of their ancestors
no matter what
their ancestors' crimes,
proud of being working class
or upper class
'though nobody boasts
a middle class birthright

don't they have accomplishments
to be proud of   situations
involving choice,
risk or responsibility

like
I'm proud of the few
occasions I've helped
ashamed
of the millions
of times I've turned away
proud
of playing my part in keeping
our love
alive

and that deserves
a moderate pat on the back
for me the rest
is gutless bullshit

Night fell like Ava Gardner's hair
an owl didn't cry
the valley didn't sleep
sheep continued to eat
bats harvested the lower depths of the sky I
kissed
you
didn't notice me

sweating
on tv the apparently innocent
condemned man spoke his lines clumsily
so whether he went to the chair or not
I didn't care

perhaps an actor
could have made me feel
those twelve high voltage years
I thought that
apart from his regular reference to God
it seemed to have made a reasonable
programme of a young thug
we should all spend time on death row
knowing
a bullet fits easier in the head
than a thought
a child easier in a cage
than a dog
night fell
like a log on a frog

Turn the page

to the same page
rage along the dull street;
it's the curtains that get me
full of themselves

the way they hang
smug
protecting secrets not worth knowing

Barely sentient
but aware to the bone
that the world will never love them
their owners starve hate and ignore themselves
I
march past
sneering at their lives

and I shove the gate and them aside
bludgeon my way up the trashcan path
turn
the lock in the key
storm the door
fall through
deliver a beer from the fridge
drop
to the couch
next to where you
would sit
with me before
we
broke ourselves

and the taste and the smell and the wound of you
lingers
and the frosted can nudges my fingers
I disappear
a tear in the sand

night falls
like a severed hand

The nation loves those wholesome
TV advertising girls

starring long before the watershed
giving oral sex
to bars of chocolate
sucking ice cream cocks
and going down
on spoonfuls of yoghurt

It's easy to imagine those lips
warm around your dick
makes me think it's time
to re-assess the British attitude
to sex

Fellatio
as family entertainment

No different from the rest
I

sidle through

tail
at half-mast

lips
poised

excuses
ready

blameless

my eyes
and life

never meet

Lingua Franca

After Sub-section (1)(b) of the amended (1988)
Section 2A of clause 10 of the Local Government act 1986
(Otherwise known as Clause 28)

Society's fist
the law
calls this *A Pretended Family Relationship*.
But I Love You. Can't they understand that?
Apparently not.

Their view is one I cannot share
having lived a prisoner for many years
in a *Pretended Family Relationship*:
the one my parents had

A killing ground they made
of every place we lived their missiles flew
the filthy names and accusations
detonating in every room
fallout landing in the opened mouths
lungs soul's eyes of my brothers and I

We lived with his violence
the lord of the realm
her twisted spine his manly work
and we his property children received our share

"Has he been hit on the head?" the doctor examined
"No!" my mother replied, lying, and I
why didn't *I* say something? The doctor
why didn't *he* ask *me*? And why were mum and I
ashamed to this quicksand conspiracy?

Back home, her tears and helplessness registered
with her sons as what a woman was for, and was;
no refuges then, low priority now, but we never forgave
her
for not rescuing us
(though he the cause, she was easier to blame)

But you and I
we make a home
wherever we are
For thirty years (and there'll be more)
we've cared for each other
helped each other
comforted, worried about and for
each other
but *they* insist that that (between two men)
is all pretend

Well, let them wallow in their cesspit of ignorance
my patience is exhausted
There are none so blind as those so cowardly
they *will* not see
and I refuse to suffer for their bigotry

Incidentally,
to staunch their self-protective flow of
"There, you see, dysfunctional family,
that's the reason";
Looking back I recognise the signs
the season
and it's clear to me I'd found the road
that led to you
long before that family warfare;
at the age of four to be precise
(and without anything 'not nice' happening)
but they can't / won't understand that
Naturally

Tomorrow I buy the gun
And kill them all

The wine is here Antonio
but where is...
ah, yes, the fear
good
you have not forgotten the fear

And the olives, you have set them well
luscious firm and juicy
the ones we left to bathe
for many days soaking in jealousy
'til their flesh acquired that bitter sweet taste

But where is the bread
Antonio, surely you have not forgotten the bread we made
from grain we grew in ourselves
made with our finest hate
grains so fine the clouds in the sky, the smoke in our souls,
the wind in our bowels are gravel sand compared, Antonio
sometimes you are less than diligent
Go now, fetch the bread we made
fetch it for our guests who hate
even in their love making

What?
Have you not seen this hate?
Revenge in every thrust. Watch him
as he ploughs her.
Listen to his mind...
"THIS
is for the PAIN", the world has given him
"THIS for the LACK of TITLE", he perceives himself allotted
"With this HURT i give, i gain my FREEDOM
Gain my SELF"

Go now Antonio
fetch the bread for our guests
who will be here soon, eager to be filled;
but remember

they must never know
never suspect
how severely we have laboured
to prepare this simple meal

but we will know
and we will realise
much
profit in this

The doorman is black and burly
This morning squarely places his pecs
and deltoid warnings in my brotherly face with
"CAN I HELP YOU"
to my baseball cap black T-shirt sandals
computer bag and cut off jeans

 I could have said
"I'm here to breakfast
with the guest in The Palace Suite
and by the way
he's worth a million at least, arsewipe!"

Instead I give him "No
Thanks"
and power through with him in tow
stalking 'till I've made the grade
receiving benediction
from the smiling cold receptionist

as two off duty business types
in T-shirts baseball caps and shorts
check their keys and joke en route
to a sweltering sauna of a Big Apple day
their pale legs gleaming
in the soft lobby gloomlight

•

This evening on the reef, Black Muscles
doesn't give a second glance
I swim in fashion with the shoal
black trousers, woven shoes, black T-shirt
nothing I can do about black face, black hands,
'black' hair, but then
the jacket whispers *"money"*
'though it came from Putney High Street
not 5th avenue

"Can I get you something...sir"
the Latino waitress in the Regency Bar
is wary
I may be the sort
who'd snort into the peanuts
mug or rape
sophisticated ears
with "*Mutha Fucka*" every other sentence
even though my private schooling
English accent reassures,
there's still a chance I'm lost uptown
searching for the servants' entrance

    "A Vodka Martini
    Dry
    Straight Up
    With An Olive"

the first of the few I'll need
to re-impose *my* day
'though I'm tempted to hurl an ashtray
smash furniture overturn tables
violently confirm her worst fears
BREAKOUT!

but I'm tired of this play
'The Constant Fight'
and abort
for another
white
night

I see my death

alone

in the middle of an indifferent
day
or night

fear
screaming
courage bleeding

nobody needing
to say good-bye

worse

the self loathing
degradation

of a death bed
conversion

to an absurd
conceit

When he arrived in America
The Indians (who
had arrived there earlier)
brought Columbus gifts
of food and artefacts

In exchange, he brought them
measles, smallpox, chains
and violent death in ways that amazed
the savages

Historically
Caucasian curiosity
kills everyone else
'though, not wishing to be
mere footnotes in this
the Indians lovingly, some say,
gave the white man
syphilis

I don't suppose
there are many
guys
who've screwed
a blond
seventeen
stone
rugby
football
front row
forward
in the passenger seat
of a small
hardtop
British
sports car

but I have

parked across
from his parents'
I'd driven him home
in time
for dinner
"They'll be waiting" he'd said
but I
couldn't
and raising
the lever
pushed
him
and the back of the seat
                    down

Stronger than me
he didn't
fight

the car
rocked
he held on
tight
pneumatic buns
urging me
in
and his tongue
searching

but I made a mistake
fell in love
with the kid inside the big
who was
already
in love
with me

believed
he'd stay
I knew
he wouldn't
knew I
couldn't
'cause I was permanent
elsewhere and anyway

he really wanted
a substitute
for his mum

and with his legs
on my shoulders
I
wasn't the one

still
It hurts to laugh
with splinters of glass in your heart

Faster than a speeding bullet
a lie becomes a truth you take
for granted
I was chewing one
as she heaved in
and heavied down

a mousy haired dangly
earringed
olive green sweatered
brown and white
chequered knee length
trousered
dirty walking booted
pig

and when she
dropped
some french-fries
on the fast food
crowded
flop house floor
her mouth said
"shit!"
with strength to startle
diners chewing
five tables away

and as we all collected
light
and life
through cost effected
molecules
of optimised
weighed and measured
air

she caught me
staring
Jesus Christ!
another New York nut
burger
flying saucer
hovering
forgotten
in my hand

and neither of us
smiled

and I

really
liked her

You know?
When you go to the super-market
and buy
a cucumber,
wrinkle free wrapped
in a tight transparent
skin

no matter how
unremarkable
the passage of the sun that day
across the nomad sky
or the traffic
floating
down the grey river road
that leads, inevitably,
here

or the crying of the "for God's sake
drop it on it's head or something!"
baby, or the breeze and the wind
with never a moment to spare
bustling about their business in the trees
en route to Patagonia, Senegal,
Slough, the Polar Playgrounds

or the Houdini birth of one of those
Australian toads
that fills itself with water
'til it's round and big
as a soccer ball burrows down
deep
in the hot desert sand
encasing itself in a slick
mucous shell
and then
sleeps

for days
weeks
months
maybe centuries dreaming of
talk show hosts
rotating, slowly, over glowing coals
alternately
smiling
and radiating concern

smiling
and radiating concern

and then, as if receiving
a signal from space
too sophisticated for our impoverished
senses to detect, some change
in the way time drinks us,
the toad pops up like *The Evil One*
in a "this ain't gonna be pretty" horror flick

No matter the "yeah yeah" of all of this,
when you pick the cucumber up
trying to scrub your mind of everything
by thinking of nothing
it's futile
'cause there's something inescapably
sexual
about this vegetable

and you want the tumescence disguised
in a plain brown wrapper
but in this enlightened era
consumers favour show and tell

so you shuffle to the check out
with all those other saps
who've got their own cucumbuses
or cucumbi
and you all know
there's something more

much more going on here
than just

salad

and the check out girl says
"how ya doin'"
and she sorts through the produce
and everything's run o' the day
'til she picks up
the cucumber

and the whole store shivers
and enters denial
but the terminal rejects everybody's code

so you all religiously avoid
eye contact
'cause you know
and you know she knows
and everyone in line knows
that she knows everybody else knows
and you all breathe a sigh of relief
when she's registered
that great green ribbed sausage
in it's added smooth 'though unlubed
protection

and thank God she's passed on
to the cereal
and the soup packets
and you pays your money
and you gets the hell out
and get home
and unpack
and put the things you've bought
away
in their allotted places
freezer, fridge, low shelf, high shelf,
drawer, cupboard, under the sink
and then

weeks later,
you open the crisper
and there it is...
the cucumber you'd forgotten all about

and trying not to pick it up
you pick it up
in your gagging hand
and the cucumber says:
"Well...friend...
it may be the beer
it may be the belly
it may be time
fear
debt
or doubt
the job
the medication
familiarity
lack of clout
it may be sadness
expectation
boredom
the war
AIDS
a lack of imagination   it may just be
you've run out of fantasy head movies
it may be you need a better class of pornography
it may be all or none of the above
but I the cucumber do not lie"

and the cucumber says in a voice of fire
to your cringing soul bathed in chilled spotlight

"face it fella,
you just can't get it up anymore";

and you close the fridge door
cross the kitchen floor
and throw yourself into the bin

Shall we taste it
Dip our fingers in
          the overflow
examine
raise   thick tears
to lips jagged with grief
                    it helps
to pass 'though not
to change the time   what else
can we do

          pavements bloom
overnight
where this rich liquid
seeps
into familiar stone

          Hopelessness
is knowing
Homo Sapiens
is God

Hearing Ben Webster's tenor soul blow
in a beer & burger joint called *The Bistro*
'cross from eighth 'n Jane street

I meet myself as a traitor to love
realising
I can't realise your face

any time I want
I can conjure Webster's smoke and glide
but you escape my need
and few functioning brain cells

I make it worse with beer
and vodka
cling to memories of photographs
to place you
in a holiday mnemonic

and it works except
you waver
blurred
and now I know for sure
it's time to go 'home'
as in, 'wherever you are'

and Billie's singing
Good Morning Heartache
wringing the world out over my beer
and you
are weeks away

I order
2 double vodkas
no tonic

my cup
is running me over

"And Labi
Siffre she's
here!" cried
the camp
v o i c e d
organ-iser
of the AIDS
charity ball.
"Is 'he' a
'she' then?"
asked the
s t r a i g h t
comedienne
n e u t r a l
voiced. "Oh
yes! She's a
great big
J e s s i e ! "
defined the
e m p h a t i c
a u t h o r i t y
who had yet
to meet the
b u t t
of his wit as
around the
corner of the
"L" shaped
r o o m
Labi Siffre paused from typing a poem into his new lap top resisted the urge to punch the guy out as once again civil-isation got the better of him and the room received his sigh with a sighhhhhhhhhhhhhhhhhhh

The meek shall inherit the dearth
Seek and ye shall be fined
Blessed are they that suborn
For they shall inherit the earth

Blessed are they that do persecute
And kill the little children
Rejoice be exceeding bad
To the poor
And thou shalt not suffer

For ye are the salt of the earth
And ye are the light of the world
Blessed are they forsworn
For theirs is the kingdom of heaven

☩

Short sighted Jesus
flawed magician
slipshod
as your father was

what point
in raising Lazarus
from the grave

while failing to repair
his hearing aid

If God is omnipotent
can do anything

And if God is omniscient
knows everything

Then
(if it also has free will)

God
is ultimately responsible

for evil

Again I throw you
                    to the sea

Again the waves
                    bring you back to me

I thank the waves
                    I thank the sea

That they know more
                    about me
                              than me

Tonight the moon reclines
In a cream coloured rocking chair
As we drive to Oyster Bay
To screw

Tomorrow
You will tell me of your dead wife
Your four sons
And thirty seven years of semi-contented lies
               In smiling colour photos of
               Commitment
               Love
               And tears falling
               from the backs of your eyes
               To your child's secret heart

You are very, very;
Large enough to worry unarmed gang members
No one would think of queer-bashing you
Four foot wide, six foot two
               But with my tongue
               In your mouth
               You kiss
               Like I was saving your life

Lacking details, yes,
But recognising longing
I try to make up for the years you've missed
But we are slightly out of sync
You don't know much of how to do
And unbeknown to you
I haven't slept in thirty six hours
Yet I make you helpless
Three hundred pounds of strength
At my behest

In the morning after photos
Of your grown up sons
One of whom I would have chased
(Had he been in the bar last night)
A smaller version of you
With something of *her* face
Your fair haired wife
Just less than beautiful
Much more than pretty

We share the cool of your blue-green kitchen
Over instant coffee saved by the trees in your garden
Reminding me of home I ask
"Do you have squirrels here?"
"Lots of 'em", you say
You'd shoot them if you had a BB gun
And smile shamefaced in answer to my wagging finger

Standing back in my head
I want to protect you
As you sit beside me filling the room
                And telling me of the shrink
                Who doubted you were gay
                When you asked for help
                Just before your wedding day

Over bagels and lox, my anger grows
While you paint your life with directorships
Chairmanships
Of worthy causes, businesses you ran
                Respected by your friends who, you say,
                Consider Gays in positions of authority
                Give inappropriate signals to the young;
                The world as always run by cowards
                Like anti-Semitic Christians
                Lacking balls enough
                Or just too dumb to see the joke

You have beautiful, heavy, soft furred hands
And big flat feet pointing outwards as you walk
Now and then as we talk I hold your hand
As you drive me to my home away from home you find
This being pursued by young
(in my case *younger* men)
Has brought you to renewed self-
Confidence
                    And now you want to find commitment
                    Man to man
                    I caution
                    Against rushing into things
                    So close to bereavement

You request and get my phone number
Angle over to be kissed
The native saves the giant explorer parked
In hostile main street daylight passers by
                    I oblige
                    Tasting you
                    For the last time.

Floating   in this foreign bed
with you snoring   me listening
to the rain playing
on the courtyard paving
where three dozen bicycles for hire
never tire reminiscing
about bottoms I wonder
is this the way a grown man
should spend irreplaceable time

Of course it is   and
tomorrow morning we two
will join their conversation

Spent   spread eagled in this foreign bed
made home temporarily
exhausted by you, I
listen to the water glistening
off your bouncing body, lucky bathroom,
as you shower the Copenhagen rain
still sings in the pedalled courtyard
as once again I'm much too tired
for breakfast

In parallel companionship touching thighs
our shadows hide in bohemian grass
on Roskilde shore with four pastel ponies
at the waters edge shifting scenery I'm writing
a verse with you reading an unkind paper
telling us how our travellers cheques
are worth much less and the restaurant boat
across the bay steams out from the harbour
and the ponies play
nip and duck and run I wonder   will we see
herons today

"You'll never be as good a poet as Bukowski"
said the mirror trying to make me cry
but I got angry
which is easier
inside

a buzzard passed the bedroom window
took me high above the valley
with its sentinel trees and two clouds
like one
of the gophers from that old cartoon
where the gophers
speak
in upper class English accents
and drink tea

Peter brought me a better mood
with a kiss
and a cup of Earl Grey
Love and poetry the only things
that make me smile these days

and he went downstairs to mind our guest
from his life in the army
a Scot from Australia who last night
laughing reminiscing raised
an unloved regiment
"the shirt lifters"

then
red faced
looked at me realising
he'd said it in the
"watch your backs boys!" voice
he'd use with his mates ('real men') back home;
'real men' have so much to prove

meanwhile

I drank the tea
looked out through the window
no sign
of the buzzard
but the trees kept on
                    marching
                        down
                            the hill

So Billie played the singing maid
and Louis was the trumpet playing butler
in the movie "New Orleans"
to make the white folks look superior
waste of time / not even close
you can't hide genius
by dressing it in servant's clothes

besides
the cookies blew their cover
saying things like
"Do you sing the blues because you're sad?"
Must be ten thousand miles of out-takes somewhere
with Billie and Louis cracking up

•

Smooth as a leopard in a leopard tree
the first of the cool sax pioneers
was Lester Young
who was never young
and always looked so eeeaaazzzyyy
in control man, hat 'n smoky joe, no jive
in those eyes making love
on a bed of blue notes
with Lady Day

•

Why didn't Lester marry Billie
It could have been so different
maybe
a happy ending 'stead of that parade
of hoods 'n hustlers stealing her money
beating her up

And while we're here:
Why didn't Powell 'The Thin Man'

(William that is, not Bud the pianist)
marry Marilyn, like she asked him;
but he
thought he was too old and she
fell
to the Kennedys

•

You got me Billie, when I heard you sing
"For all we know"
you killed that thirteen year old boy stone dead
I'm dying still

Before you did, really sick
the cops strolled in
no grapes or flowers
but silver bracelets
as a gift
for shooting up in your hospital room;
what better place?

still
no one can hurt
a dead nigger

so you escaped
finally
the winner

Six Wall Street clones
on the Sheraton steps
survey an array of stretched limos   are these
the mannequins that make the world
go round, as scientists explain how the planet
spins
slowly   slowly   slower every day

Even here on the hundred and sixtieth floor
we've learned to drink urine
eat excrement   superior
filters and bubbles
are standard at this level
Pigs
at an agricultural show
one hundred and sixty floors below
refuse to drink
city water
and lunch here
smells suspiciously
of someone else's

•

Denied, some say,
choosing to deny these choices,
professional beggars rattle
McDonalds paper cups
sometimes receiving
more than loose change, I
gave a dollar
and would have even if he hadn't said
"I don't do drugs
        'n' I don't drink
                I'm just hungry man..."

"Take the money" I thought
" 'n get yourself high,
get some alcohol man
get some drugs inside you

if we was reversed I'd be stoned
every God Damned night
every God Damned day
any which any how
any God Damned way I could

and don't fool yourself man
there's no up here-abouts
there's no way we'd want you
if you did straighten out

just be tidy
and don't die
where we have to see

It's bad enough
I can't stop
seeing
how easily
you
could be me"

(SU)
R E A
L I S M

Courtesy of Hieronymus Bosch
it's Christ on a fifteenth century Zimmer
A glimmer of hope for the maimed by nature
chained to the railings outside empathy .
Had Jesus had courage and foresight to be
a Mystic-Spastic-Cystic Fibrosic-
Downs Syndrome-
Spina Bifida-
Autistic
Spittle Spreader,
perhaps the rest of us
might have got the message

Like the smile on a killer dolphin's face
clichés cling to the corner table
where the lovers, leaning over waning coffee, plot
the shotgun shedding of his brutal wife
her frigid husband
some dependent parents (never there
when they were needed) who now
"...don't want to be a burden but..."

I stroll over to suggest additional targets:
Religious leaders *not* living in poverty
DJs who speak
And people who *tell* you when you ask "how are you?"

We make a list in an A4 note pad
The first ten pages fill
like an open wound

•

Voodoo dolls in the window seat
the two hundred fifty pound Frau From Hell
(a vulture / hippopotamus hybrid)
is Laurel'd and Hardy'd to her dry husk husband

No word between them for the past fifteen minutes
they favour my looks, the book I'm reading,
the way I'm breathing, the melt in the mouth
ham and cheese omelette I'm eating, the house
wine I ordered, my tourist map, my woolly hat
on the floor by my rucksack
with disdain

I
imagine *them*
screwing *like lions*
Sand from the bedroom floor
stuck to his bony butt

she likes to ride on top, head back, jaws twitching,
hardy savannah bushes on either side of his hips
clutched in her hands for leverage –YYYEEESSS!!!

•

As it squats and squeezes
in ecstatic congress
to the pissed-on-pissed-off pavement
none of this breezes the gargoyle Griffon
A sphincter on bandy coffee table legs
no big bang, this small Belgian Bulldog delivers
a dark brown spiral galaxy as if
from an icing bag held by the chef
at Maison Fou Fou

And the cop in the car by the metro stairs
at the squashedface dog on the job
And it's owner, the cop and the squashedface dog,
deaf to the pavement's legitimate grievances,
turn a blind eye to the natural flow
I make a mental note
to be careful when I leave

•

The natural flow is mine of course
a Negro scribbling on the Champs Écrivais
where this documenting things I've seen
and experienced,
as if they'd really happened,
is a drug which dulls the pain only
with another one

but that's ok
'cause walking jaunty through the rain
here comes a chubby Griffon I'd
like to roam
With a serious gaze and a brioche nose
his bushy moustache is red and wet
standing out proud of his childbearing lips
and his grey, duffel coat hood

I gather him up and fly to our battle bed
of ambushes, parleys, and breathless surrendering,
winning it all by losing everything
to the grasping fingers, the furry belly,
the tongue, the heavy thighs, the sex
is wonderful

as I chew on a third
not the last
breakfast cognac

and listen
to my eyes

and excrete
more words

In the morning
when the polychlorinated byphenyl sea
rolls out over my tongue and flounders
muddle my brain
timid envoys venture north
to reconnoitre

the lay of the land is happily
you
naked enough at the bedside
an archangel made
of marshmallow stepping stones
reminding the men in their foxholes
of their teddy bear status in the nursery

it's an everytime anytime
dry through the storm as toast warm
and with death and taxes a little bit smug

playing possum in tropical waters
I morph
to an octopus
faithful you stick to the script,
with a few ad libs, win a golden globe
as the monster who fought like hell
successfully fell at the first huddle
tough   nearly all the way home

The Charred Meat in this Buchenwald oven is
"COME AND GET IT"
and we do

the day the night by rhyming
moon with June
the Oberstürmfuhrer's cat
by killing another plump rat
The woman does it with a blade of ice
        cuts
photon thin slices of every day pain
made extravagant
by diligence, and dedication

Eyes bigger than my stomach
I pile my platter high with excess
and stuff my face and body full
from a feast irresistible to the common man
we
self-replicate
in a comedy that cannot be made
        "uplifting"

that story, of the brutalised, the dehumanised
who endure with a dignity we
impertinently drape
around our ready to wear shoulders,
that simplistic ballad to
"the indomitable human spirit"

is a tale worth telling to the children
who, for the sake of all, must be given hope
        without lies

but in this crevasse
we who have destroyed hope by living
beyond childhood
perpetuating us by teaching them salvation

almost entirely made
of lies

we who blame ourselves for naught
are responsible for naught
have banished shame, embarrassment even,
as we speak in tongues of fire praising
the quality of self-portraits
(commissioned by ourselves)
we deserve the version in which we are not
ennobled by *their* suffering

·

Nobody speak here
The air is a discord
Words would be, these words are,
an insult almost as gross as this place,
a centre of excellence designed
by the finest in their field
in celebration
of waste disposal and recycling

One stage in the process challenges here
a superb example of conceptual art
taller than a basket ball super star
a mound
of loose-limbed
naked
white bodies
carved solid with rigor mortis it captures
an absolute suppleness
embarrassing
to our finest gymnasts

these figures have been
fundamentally
relaxed

but the histories they bring, move us to tears
too late to do more than incite

the reflexive murder of a death camp guard
who sleeps untroubled in a bath of water clear
as the option
of being ostracised to the Russian front
for not being one of the lads
(did no one at Nuremberg cite peer pressure
as a mitigating factor)

another has escaped cleverly by suicide
no signs of anguish on either one

while that which comforts me
is after all
self-serving
a well rehearsed ad lib
a prior engagement
conveniently remembered
"I'd love to,
but I must grieve.
Call me, we'll do lunch sometime"

Yes, I cheered
as the tank swerved
to avoid the youth idealised
in Tiananmen square
but I soon enough changed channels
to an alternative source of entertainment

For example:
This pyramid of human bones
like jungle-drum beaters in a white man's cartoon
of the noble savage
It fails to inspire mountain climbers

"I hate pictures like that"
a passer-by says

"I can't face the world that way"

A handsome galleon Afrikan woman
skin shining melanin strength   hair
ready to bind
told me one evening, "You blacks in the west
(American, British) know nothing
don't you know
what we call you
back home?"

and she loaded her tongue and fired
"Niggers" she said

"We call you Niggers"

I guess she'd meant to hurt me
she was certainly angry
indignant at my alignment of racism
shoulder to shoulder – with homophobia

and she threw the usual GIGO stuff
about nature and choice and The Lord
and seemed *the most* upset
'cause I wasn't effeminate

almost as if
by *not* limping my wrists
I was somehow being dishonest   she said,

"It's different for you
If you're Gay you can lie

If you're black
you can't hide"

and
almost in admiration I smiled
'cause for that moment at least
she was unique

colour blind

and because in society
the soul
is on the outside

and because
like her
I've nowhere to hide

she was angry
embarrassed
afraid
because

I
won't
lie

GIGO: Garbage In Garbage Out.

First I
fucked you

Then you
fucked me

I feel
sorry
for straights

Having only
half
a sex life